ne

Driving in the Dark

Jean Stevens is a poet, playwright and actor. Her poems have appeared in *London Magazine*, *Stand*, *The North*, *Mslexia*, *The Honest Ulsterman*, *Other Poetry*, *Smoke*, and the *Bridport Prizewinners' Anthology (2016)*, and have been broadcast on BBC Radio 3 and 4. She is a past winner of the Yorkshire Post Poetry Prize and the Leeds Libraries Writing Prize, and was recently shortlisted for the Poetry Business Pamphlet Competition and *The Rialto* Poetry Prize.

Jean's plays have been performed at Derby Playhouse, the Edinburgh Festival, Harrogate Theatre and West Yorkshire Playhouse, and her stand-up comedy script won the Polo Prize at London's Comedy Store. As a professional actor she has credits for stage, film and television.

jeanstevenspoet.co.uk

An exciting contemporary voice full of warmth and charm
Daljit Nagra

A sure hand
Ian McMillan

Thoughtful, sensitive and well-crafted
Amy Wack

Also by Jean Stevens

Poetry

Performances (Pica Press 1999)
Undressing in Winter (Matador 2008)
Beyond Satnav (Indigo Dreams Publishing 2016)

Plays

Twockers, Knockers and Elsie Smith (1997)
Journey (1998)
both published by Smith and Kraus, USA

DRIVING IN THE DARK

Jean Stevens

Naked Eye Publishing

© Jean Stevens 2018

All rights reserved

Book design and typesetting by Naked Eye

ISBN-13: 9781910981047

www.nakedeyepublishing.co.uk

Acknowledgements

Some of these poems were first published in *Stand*, *The North*, *Mslexia*, *Smoke*, *Orbis*, *Acumen*, *Cake*, *The High Window Journal*, *Dream Catcher*, *Artemis* and *Brittle Star* magazines and the *Bridport Prizewinners' Anthology* (2016).

Contents

I Another Place

Cartref..13
Mediobogdum Roman fort..14
Ada Martindale's..15
Local hills..16
If it snows..17
Hidden..18
Northern garden...19
Like smoke...20
Jackdaws..21
Viewpoint...22
Googling the nightingale..23
Woodland stories..24
The power of water..25
Black ice...26
Kite-flying in Morecambe..27
Miners..28
Carrying the boat...29
Another country...30

II Another Life

After the Manchester bomb..33
Jumble sale...34
Fell farmer..35
Beatrice..36
Belonging...37
Picnic..38
Café Royal...39
Charabanc..40
Skeleton..41
Brown rat..42
When I was immortal...43
This is the man...44
Nickname...45
If I use my mind's eraser on your house..............................46

The first hours..47
The Walking Madonna...48
Beethoven in Burnley...49

III Another Love

Listening to the thunder..53
His office..54
Ghost..55
Stalker..56
Snoring...57
He used to..59
Returning without you..60
The high wood...61
Attermire Scar..62

IV Another Day

Driving in the dark..65
That night..66
White dawn..67
Coming from sleep..68
Blue..69
That spring...70
At the top of the hill...71
High summer in the park...72
We left the horses on the beach...73
A bottle on a glass table..74
Slip...75
The movement of air..76
Journey..77
Homeward commute..78
Wham...79
Another dawn..80

I

Another Place

Cartref

'D'you know what it means, Cartref?'

I was shopping with a bag I bought in Laugharne
to hold books of poems when on that first
holiday alone and too distracted to question
the unfamiliar word printed on the hessian.

Weighed down with groceries, I thought
back five years to Dylan's house where
his recorded voice resonating *Do Not Go Gentle*
sent me running to the estuary's hungry shore
to walk and walk, to see what he saw

from the boathouse - lapwings, heron,
otters, seals - and to try to see what more he found
beneath the cold waves, beneath everything.
I thought, too, of that day in New York when
he was only thirty-nine …

'It means *home*.'
I wondered why I hadn't found out before
when, even after five years, nowhere feels like home
to me, and I still look for solace in words.

Mediobogdum Roman fort

Along the seeming edge of the world
fringing the chasm of Hardknott Pass
through chicanes and paperclip bends
slick with skidded mud
we struggled to the top
of England's steepest road
and thought of five hundred cavalry there
feeling the stab of the cold.

Against the swoop and curl
of the fells, between loaded clouds,
raw sun lit the ruins that still command
the marshy grass where remnants
of leather tunics, shoulder belts
and scattered shoes were found -
two thousand years
folded into the land.

Ada Martindale's

Out on the North York Moors
on a black cloaked night
I passed through crossroads
whose signs had been uprooted

and don't remember how
I came across the isolated house
with her name as licensee
carved over a door which led

straight into her front room,
low-ceilinged, whitewashed, sparse,
where five men who looked as if
they'd done a bloody good day's work

sat at a scarred pine table
and Ada, weathered as landscape,
appeared at the door of a scullery
where bottles shone on a granite slab.

I asked for a pint of ale and we sat
companionably at the table though
I don't recall that anyone spoke.
They sat and smoked and now and then

one of the workers opened the door
and peed outwards into the night.
The decades rolled away
pulling me back to a solid core.

Out on the moors again I wanted to walk,
to be driven by darkness and need,
whiplash rain, a strong wind,
cold that seeks your skeleton.

Local hills

They are not mountains
but have the look of them
even to the caps of snow
along ridges sharp as a stage set
against a cyclorama sky
and with clefts and hollows
that baffle the eye. Only the trees
find out how deep they go.

At night a winter moon
like a snowball thrown to the sky
creates on their slopes
the white peaks of Kilimanjaro,
Fuji, Everest.

If it snows

she will take the old road
past the ruined barn
watching her boots tackle
muddy ruts left by tractors

she will trudge the tilting fields
and climb the hill
watching the flakes float
onto skeleton hawthorn
blink her lashes free
of frost, welcome the cold

and she will clamber over ancient
stiles, edge through narrow gaps
and up through cloisters
of beech, deeper and deeper
into the wood's silence

hoping this time
she'll reach the clearing where
all the tricky patterns meet.

Hidden

When I first came here
I was overawed by
the billow of hills rising
above my cottage,
wondered what was hidden
behind the sycamores
fringing their curves.

I climbed until all breath
had gone from me,
struck off the path,
reached the top and, as if I were
someone else, looked down
on the tiny house and garden
of my own miniature life.

I discovered a barn
tucked away in the folds
behind the trees,
spoke to a lone farmer,
patted his dog,
stood absorbing the place
till my body cramped

but the hills remain a mystery,
lifting like dolphins
into another element.

Northern garden

Jutting above the hedge
that surrounds an ordinary little plot
the builders left in chaos,
a tropical palm struggles
to love its northern garden.

It's been wrapped in fleece
which already hangs in grubby shreds
where wind and rain have draggled through.
But the tree has grown over the months
I've watched the gardener at work

attempting to bring Eden here.

Like smoke

In the time it takes to light a cigarette
I glimpse a château I never knew was there.
When I blink it seems to be a farmhouse
with perhaps a dovecote on the side.

My feet scrape on the roots of trees
not yet in leaf; a hard winter
has made new gaps through which this croft,
castle, whatever, calls across the open field.

Air hangs as if the frost has halted it
and, though my cigarette is doused now,
my breath is still like smoke trying
to find the language of signalling.

An old woman hunched against the cold
walks through the long grass towards the building.
She turns and raises her hand. Is she warning me
to stay away or beckoning me on?

Jackdaws

They came mob-handed that year
when we lived in the old barn,
waking us every dawn rollocking
at the window frames, errant beaks
ripping out strips of wood till I fretted
the glass would craze.

A yob leading a teenage gang
the man from the council said,
setting a trap with an egg as bait.

Next day we saw the rogue bird
among broken shell, agitating
his wings but lifting barely an inch
before he hit wire mesh.
He fluttered and fell, fluttered
and fell, over and over trying to fly.

A bird being itself made a coward of me.
You were the one who went out,
got blood on your clothes.

Viewpoint

On rainy days when I look out
Pendle Hill is no longer there,
but in sun it bosses the horizon, changes
the light and shade round every bend.

Its eastern slope watched over
my childhood and teens,
was always the first familiar thing
I saw when I came home.

Now I view it from the west
I have reversed my life.

Googling the nightingale

They don't fly this far north
so I googled the nightingale
I'd never seen or heard:
plush in my chair I was warm
and dry, no need of binoculars
or a hide, while from a Constable
landscape came four full minutes
of bird and song - and I fidgetted,
yawned, looked at my watch.

That evening at dusk I put empty
milk bottles out on the step,
picked up the litter - fag ends,
half-eaten chips, a dirty lager glass -
saw that someone had
peed down the wall
and out of the coming dark
a blackbird sang - as a rainbow
might sing if a rainbow could.

Woodland stories

Tonight the moon is caught
in the branches of the beech
whose bony-fingered silhouette recalls
dark woodland stories heard as a child.

Wolves circle
the white lit icy garden

noses lifted towards the sky
throats flexing

to howl some fierce song
and loosen the strings

that tether me to this world
and all its trappings.

The power of water

Those days of the floods
I became an acolyte
in the world of drains,
found a steel grid, forced out
by the rush of wet, drifting
across the drowned lawn
like a miniature leaking raft,
another glued to its outlet
by a cement of slurry
beech leaves and clay
thick as treacle.

I waded up the road,
now an unstoppable stream,
and saw a drain cover
shaped like a frisbee
lifted by the thrust of the flood
and dancing on top of a fountain
whose waters frothed and curled
like the feathers the Black Prince wore.

Black ice

A country road at midnight
  the car hits black ice

stamp on the brakes
  wrench into reverse
switch off the engine
  drag on the handbrake

career even faster
    ricochet
off a new Mini Sports
  climb the verge
    hit a tree.

Then a touchable quiet
as if the world has stopped
and nothing can breathe.

Two large dark men
unfold from the Mini
stand like giants.
I tremble out of my Ford.

One man reaches into their car -
  to get a weapon I think

till the stereo blasts reggae
  and I join them both
dancing in drifted snow
singing *No woman, no cry.*

Kite-flying in Morecambe

Over the weekend
gales hefted rubbish bins
bowled them downhill
scattering broken glass, eggshells,
torn-up bills, final demands,

shifted to a shrieking northerly
that almost tempted me to dare it
to fling me from the pier
into a whirlpool of tides.

Monday morning
thronging the shoreline
a class brought out of school

learning, the teacher says,
about the force of air, the ways
of wind, the power of storms

but the children, who came eager
to wrestle the wind, to risk
the rolling grab of the sea,
stand drooping in the dead calm
kites dangling from idle hands.

Miners

With Orwell's romantic eye
Lawrence's nostalgia
I see them walking the morning awake
a group of *mustn't grumble* men
wearing helmets and Davy lamps.

On the well-worn path to the pithead,
I see men nip out of their houses
to join the growing procession
as a soundtrack fades in with a Welsh choir
singing *Cwm Rhondda*.

My reverie's broken by colliding rumbles
the crash of a roof caving in, the slither
down the hillside of a slagheap on the move.
All that's left are blind pit ponies, dead canaries,
silicosis, the poisonous word Orgreave.

Carrying the boat

She'd always wanted to see Alice Springs
not knowing there's hardly any water there
and they run a boat race up the dry creek
with hollowed-out boats held around their waists.

What she wanted was warmth and red soil
and never ever to see another snowman
having left him constructing yet one more
in the frozen Alaskan wilds.

All she wanted was the sound of running water
filling the hot creek or melting the ice
of a life as dry as her hollowed-out self.

Another country

Across the water
the city we explored
looks small as
a model village:

hills, sand,
a lit resort
and in the distance
another country.

We are somewhere
both foreign and familiar
and in one glance see
where we've been
and where we've yet to go.

II

Another Life

After the Manchester bomb

Josie's been doing a jigsaw,
her seven-year-old eyes
focusing on bits of sky.

If you do the sky first
the rest will follow
but the blue all looks the same

and today she's clumsy -
there are pieces on the floor.

She kneels, picks up half a face,
its one eye staring at her,
part of an arm,
some bits she can't identify.

She'll come back
to the scattering of people.
The sky's the thing
and now she can see
differences in the blue,
a grey cloud here
a streak of light there
a tiny bird lifting up to heaven
but it's still too hard on her own -

sometimes, though they often fight,
her sister Vicky helps her when she's stuck
but Vicky isn't here.

Jumble sale

In a rusty Crawford's biscuit tin,
I find a pair of pale pink ballet shoes,
a photo album labelled who, when and where -
then, at the back, an unmarked photograph
so faded I almost have to enter it to see who's there -

a sepia child, six, seven maybe, alone on a beach,
her dress white, crisp, high-necked, long-sleeved,
embroidered with the elaborate tucks and folds
only starch can keep, her (surely restless) feet
in black lace-up boots. Below the frilled bonnet
her eyes are solemn, focused on the photographer.

She'd need to keep so very still. Not like a child
today leaping around in a purple and pink bikini
caught in a flash by a mobile 'phone.

Fell farmer

After she's fed the children, ferried them
to school, hung washing on the line to jump
and crack in the wind, she fettles a sheep
for showing, grapples its bulk, as she combs
thick fleece, scrubs the bold black and white
on face and legs, buffs the horns.

Not long ago she saw her cattle shot,
heaped like a battlefield, her pregnant ewes
dragged into wagons and taken to slaughter,
breathed the stink of smoking pyres,
the work of generations - her beloved
Swaledales - wiped out in hours.

To a rhythm old as mankind, she continues
to slop out shit, wade through mud, fight
disaster and disease, struggle waist deep in snow
to uncover the flock, lives through lambing,
shearing, stone-picking after the plough,
and drives the tractor like Boudicca.

She says she's gnarly now, but see her
at evening riding alone towards the high fell
half-crouched, half-standing, her boots black
with dried dung, on a quad bike covered in muck
and grease, tilting into the sunset, a disciple
of the mountain, her face made only of light.

Beatrice

Stick in hand, feet in wellies,
a young girl bringing the cows
for milking, a two-mile trek across
Cambridgeshire fields, nudging
the cattle into line, doing what
she does every day after school.

The cows trail to the swing of their
heavy load, she skips along aware
how much there's yet to do: feed her
motherless baby sister, bring water
in buckets, light the fire in the range
to heat the black-leaded stove.

Those days fold back into each other
when she tells me all this in a fading voice
as I lie on the ninety-year-old bed
cradling my mother-in-law
who is frail as a wounded sparrow
knowing it's time to go.

Belonging

He took her to the farmhouse
but it was only an address, never
a home. The barn was owned by owls,
the river by stones and trout.

The fields were owned by sheep
who scattered if she went near
and cattle loomed at her
whenever she ventured a walk.

She never liked that house
and, no matter what she did,
she was always owned by him.

Picnic

A cricket bat and ball, trodden
grass, a dragonfly kite ready
for when we'd race up the hill,
my mother unpacking the plaid rug,
cheese and tomato sandwiches,
a jam-filled sponge,
my dandelion and burdock drink
cool in a beige stone bottle

and me at the water's edge
watching with tight breath
my father, who couldn't swim,
wading thigh deep towards the far
bank to set a trapped heron free
his rolled-up trousers sopping wet
the breadth of the river between us.

Café Royal

It was the only time I saw my father embarrassed -
the restaurant was perfect in candlelight,
crisp white tablecloths like an altar,
waiters who leapt forward lighters ablaze before
he got a Woodbine from its pack, the way
the maître d' held a linen-draped bottle just so.

The menu was arty farty - meant to humiliate
and my father glanced at his hands:
had he got the dirt out of the creases,
the smell and grease of petrol from his nails?

We ate under watchful eyes but my father seemed in control.
Then, holding the bill, he looked at me with fear
in his eyes: How much? How much is it okay to tip?

Charabanc

My mother stands at the front of the coach -
she calls it a *sharrerbang* - steadying herself
by a red-nailed hand on the driver's seat
and we're on our way home from Blackpool.

Fearing what she's going to do, I shrink down
in my seat, the flush creeping up from my chest
to the top of my head, try to look as if
I've never seen this woman before.

We swing round the bends as she sings
'I'll take you home again, Kathleen'
loud and clear if not exactly in tune. All eyes
are fixed on her as she conducts a mobile choir.

She's been held back by our family view -
good things *are not for the likes of us* - and part of me
wants to shout 'Look at her, look at my Mum,
she's been longing for limelight all her life.'

Skeleton

At the foot of Malham Cove
lost among stones and grass
through snow, wind and rain
the skeleton whitens

before a scorch of light
casts red, pink, yellow
returns flesh to skull, tibia, ulna
washes blood through veins.

The chest rises and falls
eyelids tremble

clothes fly back to the body.
He stands in the fell-runner's boots
he loves and the college outfit
his mother scrimped to buy.

Then he's up top again giddy
peering down the long, stony way
toes wavering over the edge
till he breaks the trance
and slides his feet back, back,

back to the pedals on his bike
going widdershins down the lane
to the cottage and kitchen table
back to the simple choice
of what this day is for.

Brown rat

The poison's hidden in food.

Is the creature
curled in a corner,
or vomiting, gasping
for water, running
in panicked circles?

On freezing nights
he came for warmth to my
pious compost heap

fluffy chestnut fur,
bright eyes, lively feet
that sculpted the waste
for a family nest.

I'm paying someone to kill him,
him and his kind.

When I was immortal

I drove a souped-up car
a hundred miles an hour
down switchback lanes

walked a deep chasm
on a bridge made more of air
than of its rotting timbers

with no insurance, seat belt
or life raft, flew in a tiny
rusted plane with a learner pilot

without saddle, helmet
or thought, rode a horse
as wild as Pegasus

in the dead hours in Soho
wandered into a cul-de-sac
and let a stranger kiss me.

This is the man

who when he was fourteen
worked his passage to Oz on a cargo boat,
chafed the flesh off his hands on wet ropes,

slithered across a tilting deck, learned to smoke
and drink, broadened his stock of oaths,
sheared recalcitrant sheep, and herded cattle

across the outback under an unforgiving sun,
working his stallion back and forth like someone
playing a violin, slept with only a horse blanket

between him and the still hot soil. Now, fighting
muscle disease at work in him, he takes twenty
minutes to dress and, when he gets his breath back,

sits on the bed, smoothing difficult trousers and shirt.
But yesterday I saw him riding his bike
under an English sun, not knowing he was

observed. Racing downhill, he took his
feet off the pedals, fingers off the handlebars,
hurtled over the cobbles whooping like a child.

Nickname

Among the worn-out phrases -
architect designed, executive,
superbly presented, bijou - was one
unique to him. From tiny terrace

to mansion house, they all had *maximum sky*
which became our nickname for him
when he helped us through several moves
with his *trust me I'm an estate agent* grin.

He drove a red convertible Jag, lived in
a *renovated farmhouse,* had a four-by-four
and a stable of horses, settled we thought
till he walked to the top of the hill

with its *uninterrupted views*
carrying a length of skipping rope
and chose the oak the children climbed
the branch they used for a swing.

Jonathan, Jonathan, Jonathan,
we wish you *maximum sky.*

If I use my mind's eraser on your house

the whole street is gradually rubbed out, turned to rubble,
then back to the green that came before, and it's as if I never
stood outside clutching my bottle of red wondering if I dare
go in and risk not passing muster with your friends.

If there were no house, you couldn't have lived there
and, if you hadn't lived there, in a town you chose at random,
we never would have met and that night
I wouldn't have felt so awkward and out of place.

And if there were no house, I'd not have seen the way
you looked directly at me as you picked her from the crowd
and invited the younger, brasher blonde into your bed.

But I want to re-draw everything, brick by brick, tile by tile,
and re-live the time when the party had yet to come, the time
when there were just the two of us - long before the blonde.

The first hours

In the first hours of motherhood
I wanted to do away with walls
run wild for miles.

In the first hours of motherhood
I swelled with milk
built a den from blankets.

In the first hours of motherhood
I gained muscle and sinew
knew what it was to prowl the night.

In the first hours of motherhood
I grew claws
learned the language of tigers

planned how I would kill
anyone who threatened you.

The Walking Madonna
Sculpture by Elisabeth Frink in Salisbury Cathedral Close

Not the blue-clad, doe-eyed Mary,
not the Mary with a halo pressing her down.

This Mary strides along as if she'd walk the plain,
the bronze folds of her dress clinging
to well-muscled legs and shoulders,
carrying her load of history right to the water's edge.

This Mary's seen what life can do,
heard taunts like *slag* and *slut*,
remembers how she was torn apart
by what had been and was to come

as she gave him life among the cow dung
under a dirty sky. How the animals
ate the afterbirth and were her only allies.

Beethoven in Burnley
after Tom Pow

He's strolled into the little room
behind what used to be the tripe shop,

watches the kids loll on the floor,
bang on purple drums, clash red cymbals,

peep out notes on yellow plastic recorders.
Beethoven's enjoying himself for he's young

his hearing's sharp as hell and these kids are something else.
Though he's strangely dressed and no lover of children,

the helpers don't need to shield them - he's humming along
to their tune. He's going to be old, profoundly deaf,

crabby with the arrogance of careless genius,
but today he takes music down to its roots.

Watch him conduct with a bright green plastic
drumstick, note after random note.

III

Another Love

Listening to the thunder

Once, listening to the thunder
of water sluicing down Victoria Falls
you told me - your voice low, its cadence
underpinning that compelling roar -
that when you were seven, someone launched
you, a non-swimmer, into a flooded fenland river,
your backside wedged in a lorry tyre,

and sent you rudderless towards the weir
whose rushing sound came back to you

and I could only watch, unable to rescue you
from your memory of the Great Ouse
years before, the Zambezi's ceaseless
clamouring that day, or the future
storm in your lungs and throat
when you were finally pulled under.

His office

Because we left so much
unsaid and you're no longer
in the house, I travel to your office
through streets and buildings
hollow as a Hollywood set.

Marble and glass are slovenly
now, and I can't find
your marked slot, so stop
in the visitor car park, where
newsprint somersaults in the wind.

The lift is stuck between floors,
there are pock marks on the stairs,
the outer office phones are dead,
computers blank as wiped blackboards
and over all a dirty dishcloth smell.

I sit in your chair, feel the dry
touch of paper yellowing
on the dusty desk, see there's no bulb
in your anglepoise lamp -
a monk's cowl without a face.

Ghost

I thought I saw and heard you,
dark haired, well set, librarian specs,
arguing shades of meaning
packed in a word, singing tenor
in Fauré's *Requiem*, creating
a chequerboard of herbs and turf along
the borders of our garden, raising
a fizzing glass to our last anniversary.
Have you thought you saw and heard me,
brindle haired, angular, green eyes
flashing as I argued back, reading
my poems out loud, picking sprigs
of rosemary to sprinkle on veggie bake,
and holding my empty glass?

Stalker

Although you didn't know it
he was walking right behind
like a stalker who's located you
on your mobile phone, hid himself
up a tree, dodged behind a wall,
watching you all the time.

What he planned for me
was a tarnished mirror
where the door was reflected opening
and closing with never a shadow of you
though flowers appeared
in their brief, bright moments.

I remember that hall
how the light came and went
creating scenes in the glass -
you with your briefcase, tired as hell,
you holding an injured bird,
you in your wellies, dripping wet -
till he grabbed you by the throat.

Snoring

(i)

I wake to the sound of snoring
nothing like the usual snoring
when I shout *Wake up you bugger*
and attempt to turn you over.

No, I wake to a sound that grips
snore, rattle, gasp in its fist
deep and going deeper. *Wake up,*
you must wake up.

This isn't me messing about
saying a marriage can founder
on snores. This is it.

This is me saying forgive me
this is me saying I love you
now when it's far too late.

(ii)

This is me saying I love you
now when it's far too late.

I mean, love's ridiculous
when you've lost your hair,
your waistline, your hearing,
and your sweating stains the bed;

when the bags under my eyes
have bags themselves, and my
boobs are moving towards the floor.
But come back and I vow

with my bare hands I'll scrub
your skidmark underpants
till I grow raddled and sore
immersed in water that scalds.

He used to

leave door after door open,
would open the fridge, take out the milk,
fill a jug, put on the kettle, yawn
in the corner, and I'd be gritting my teeth
Close the bloody door.

My frustration peaked
after he left the gate to the garden
swinging back and forth, and the kids
at the age to run laughing under a bus.

A wardrobe, a cupboard, a drawer,
he left it open, but the house
is dead quiet now and I've taken to
doing the rounds at night, lifting
latches, placing wedges,
flinging the windows wide.

Returning without you

I expect difference
but Tintoretto's nailed light stuns
as it always has, Shakespeare's
ghost as ever walks the Rialto
and touts approach but, now
I'm alone, no-one offers me a rose.

In St. Mark's Square the orchestra
still plays Vivaldi and, lost
in each other, a young couple waltz
then stand entwined to hear the violins.
In seconds, a figure black as death
has emptied their pockets and bags.

The high wood

I planned to welcome you to my new garden
from where we would have looked up
to the calling hills, knowing that's where
we'd walk but taking time to appreciate you could.

You feared the risky operation, yet were excited
picturing what it might be like at last
to have the breath to tramp for miles,
watching your Yorkshire Terrier run wild.

At the top of the steepest rise I would
have shown you the high wood where birdsong
makes the following silence richer, and the air fizzes
with insects among chamomile and clover.

We would have spread our coats where two drystone walls
meet by a dip in the land. It would have been ordinary
yet amazing and I would, perhaps, have said what I never
said before because the time was always wrong.

Attermire Scar

at my age I've fallen in love again
fallen in love with the bones of this place

there are trees, grass, drystone walls
but it's the hidden skeleton that draws me

here on the fault line
between limestone and millstone grit

no-one should flirt with these hills

rising in crags over range after range
of reefs, coral slowly grown
in the shallows of an ancient sea

and deep underground giving way
to potholes, caves, cathedrals
shaped by water

this is love hardened
and knapped by stone

IV

Another day

Driving in the dark

This unlit country lane
is a woodcut in different blacks
the ink of midnight
rough coal of tree trunks
gloss of wet tarmac.

My headlights make prayer flags
of the torn paper caught in twigs
and now and then in the undergrowth
catch the gleam of an eye.

I'm moving away from all I know,
gripped by conversations
about those who've travelled
this way and seen a woman

suddenly there in front of them
her fingers agitating the air,
and spoke of crashing off the road
or of driving right through her.

I peer ahead hoping to see,
perhaps, a light in a lone farmhouse,
a junction in the distance, but in front
of me there's only this dark road.

That night

It was my three a.m.,
your afternoon, when your text
shocked me awake
to the word *malignant*
which spread its meaning
through my own lungs
as I left the hug of the duvet
and stood in my thin shift
against the window's cold.

I looked out at the small lights
fighting the dark and wished
my message to you through space:

Send the sun round the earth to me
and I'll ship you the crescent moon
to carry you in its curve
as I first held you
when you came to me
through the pains.

White dawn

Untouched except
by blackbirds' feet, snow
lies like an ermine coat
across the garden -
even the sun emerges white.

On a day like this I stood
in the lash of the wind
holding a handful of frosted
soil, deep dug earth
open in front of me

and now on this
drained morning
dare for a moment
to wonder what it's like
under stone, grass and soil
out of the light, dissolving
to the whiteness of bone.

Coming from sleep

a gradual remaking of the world
first the eyes open
pupils adjust to day

I wipe the moisture
from inside the window
there's mist
heavy on the hillside
morning gleam
of lit windows
the open arms of trees

and from behind the crag
apricot and yellow streaks
slowly lift the sun

I conjure sheep
out of the distant haze
twigs on hawthorns

if I concentrate I might
myself create the leaves

Blue

There's a hint of blue in the drizzle grey
of the sky - not enough to mean hours of sun -
it's going to be a day of distances,
everything seen through a haze of rain
wondering which is more unreal
the viewer or the viewed.

I wander out with bare feet
welcome the sting of gravel, the trickle
of blood when I scrape my toes
on a tumble of twigs torn
from the rowan by a thin wind.

On this day of question marks
do I imagine the slap of waves
hidden behind the mist,
the smell of salt on the air?

I scatter handfuls of broken bread;
above me the beech tree flexes its wings.

That spring

we were like swallows returning
except that swallows know
they're home and we never did.

It wasn't that we'd left a nest or looked
to build one; it was that we felt
this was the place that called us.

We knew the hills, the valleys, the river,
as if they were mapped inside us
though we hadn't trodden this land before.

We had nomad feet but our minds
wanted us to settle like the swallows
if only for a season. We never

worked out whether we belonged
or were strangers; didn't even know
if we had the right to be there.

But every spring I miss those hills,
I miss who we were, and am
not ready for what we have become.

At the top of the hill

where wind meets wind
and the curlew makes its nest
is coarse green moorland
spiked with heather and gorse.

You can lie unseen and look up
at the blue and white concert
playing notes across the sky
your body heavy on the grass

but your imagination rising
to the kestrel hanging overhead,
as you taste the milky sap

of white clover. Here is where you
had your first kiss, and where
you scattered your mother's ashes.

High summer in the park

Bare-chested men
lean lazy on their elbows,
women tuck their skirts high
flirting with the sun,
children laugh, shout, chase dogs
down the sloping grass,
racquets thwack tennis balls,
small flotillas crowd the lake
and, in the blue,
just one cloud heavy with rain

then a blast of music

gone quickly as it came

and in the sudden silence
a child stands frozen,
wasps hovering at her lips.

She drops her ice cream
which puddles to nothing
at her feet. Around her the park
resumes its lively noise.

We left the horses on the beach

and, stripping off, I raced
into the sea. Maybe because
I was naked - or on that first break
without mum and dad - I swam
on and on beyond the drag
of the waves, beyond cramp
gripping my legs, shaking off
who knows what

until I saw the tide had turned
and everyone had disappeared.

I struggled to make any kind
of stroke and hours went by
before I crawled up the beach,
grabbed my horse's reins, and stood
knowing something had changed
in me, sharp as the sand
chafing between my toes.

A bottle on a glass table

shifts facets of almost
painted light

as when yellow and pink
it lifts between folds
in the daybreak hills

or hangs blue cold
between stark branches
at frosty midnight

or on hot tarmac
conjures a shimmer of water.

All this
astonishes my eyes
after the surgeon's knife.

Slip

I think of the tall green and white jug
shaped like a bunch of celery
opening intricately at the frondy top,
and of the hands that moulded clay -
you're laughing at me now *Not clay,
you daft bugger, slip, it's called slip* -
and I slip back into your world
of red Mini teapots, sculpted seabirds,

a barbed wire crucifix, your garden
which was loved to wildness, and that day
when the dragonflies hung like lace
against the darkness of the pond,
and we lingered in the sun on the bench
you carved from fallen wood, you
before you slipped out of reach,
you showing me the red kites overhead.

The movement of air
i.m. Phil Orchard

We hold your sixtieth just as you'd planned,
overflowing dishes, bubbly on ice,
Mozart's liquid sonatas, bright sun
and just enough movement of air
to ripple the grass and bell the marquees.

I've brought angel cake and memories,
like the day I saw an injured pheasant
flapping in the road, and arrived shaken
at your door and you said *It'll die soon
and the mysterious red kites will come.*

Now I walk alone to the end of your wild
garden and sit on the bench by the pond
among flag irises and reeds,
listening to music filtered through the trees
till a reflection stirs on the water

and, high above me, a red kite rides the sky
on still wings. I watch the red-brown flashed
by white and silver, the bright yellow feet,
until with a faint sway of his tail he sails
easily out of sight, buoyant on all that air.

Journey

As I pick at bits of salad in a motorway café
my granddaughters offer me forkfuls
of burger, their eyes huge with hope
that I will love their choice.
I can't believe how strongly
my heart surges towards them.

Yesterday we travelled the same
one hundred and thirty miles the other way,
a journey they'd asked to join,
as if they recognised this push to growing up,

though last night they slept with the light on
in their great grandmother's house
after they'd seen her lowered into the dark.

Homeward commute

Dusk. Drizzle. The car radio drones
about wars, refugees, revenge.

Drivers cut in, honk, swear,
intimidate, hang on my bumpers

till on a slip road
to the thunderous motorway
the vehicle in front
slews to a sudden stop.

I stamp on the brakes, veer right,
the driver behind swerves left,
the one behind him squeals right

and all the way up
we synchronise like ballet,
forming a corset laced with cars.

Nobody's hurt, uses his horn,
or shouts red-faced.

Mirror to mirror
smiles reflect.

Wham

Wham. Every light went out
in the house, the street,
the town, the world.
I groped the rough fabric
of chairs, stubbed my toe
against the table leg,
fumbled for the cold metal key,
jabbed till it found the keyhole,
felt the weight of darkness
in the heavy door, stumbled outside

to be startled by thousands of years
of light from stars
I'd forgotten were there.

Another dawn

and still not the words for it,
not even the definition:

*when the upper edge of the
sun's disc is coincident
with an ideal horizon -*

- that slow astonishment of light
rising behind the jagged ridge
of the hill, fanning out coral, yellow,
red across the aching blue -

nothing describes
that lurch of the blood, that brief
belief in something more.

Naked Eye Publishing
A fresh approach

As a not-for-profit publisher, Naked Eye is part of the revolution. Co-existing on the newly-levelled playing field alongside the publishing multi-nationals, we prioritise literary and artistic interest. Our books are by and for creatives, intellectuals, art-lovers and bookworms - and at an affordable price. We also publish, where feasible, downloadable versions. Writers we publish do not need agents, nor do they have to financially invest, and they benefit from free global availability and distribution through our printing firm's worldwide partnerships which include Barnes and Noble, Bertrams, Gardners, Waterstones and Amazon. Using the most up-to-date print technology we publish beautiful books of old-fashioned quality.

Our current remit covers world contemporary literary fiction and poetry including new English translations; also art, photography, and our Potted Thesis series: academic theses abridged and retold in a lay-person's terms.

nakedeyepublishing.co.uk

www.ingramcontent.com/pod-product-compliance
Lightning Source LLC
Chambersburg PA
CBHW071317080526
44587CB00018B/3259